COVID-19 and Me

PAGE PUBLISHING
Conneaut Lake, PA

First originally published by Page Publishing 2024

ISBN 979-8-88654-648-4 (pbk)
ISBN 979-8-89315-619-5 (hc)
ISBN 979-8-88654-657-6 (digital)

Printed in the United States of America

COVID-19 and Me

JANETTE A. SMITH

My mommy says I can't go to school today.

She makes me go to my room and play.

I hate being in my room all day.

I have something I really want say.

I want to see my teachers today.

Mom, I don't like how you teach any old way.

I really miss all my friends.

This virus is a fool, and this is not cool.

I need my teachers—I really, really do.

What is this virus everyone is talking about anyway?

Is this why we can't go to school and out to play?

Social Distancing
6 Feet Apart

Why do we have to wear these silly old masks?

My dad keeps saying this virus won't last.

These masks keep us safe from COVID-19's deadly germs.

When we are out and about during these deadly terms.

We must all wear these silly old masks and stay six feet from others.

The love is being shielded as if there were no mothers.

So stay at home; it will do us all good.
This protection order just must be understood!
When this coronavirus passes, and it's out of sight.
We can get back to classes, and everything will be

ALL RIGHT.

So...

You must wear your mask when you are out and in class.

Please stand on the
markings on the floor.
Social Distancing
6 Feet Apart

Stay six feet from others when you are out in public.

Always wash your hands with warm water and soap.

Just

remember:

Stay safe and healthy. Follow all the rules. Especially when you are in school.

We will win this fight and kick covid out of SIGHT.

Far

far

far!

The end!

About the Author

A native of Memphis, Tennessee, author Janette A. Smith later moved to Hernando, Mississippi, where she attended Hernando Central High. After graduation from high school, she moved to Detroit, Michigan, where she attended Wayne County Community College and Wayne State University, where she earned her bachelor of science degree in special education and her master's degree in elementary education. After thirty-two years of teaching grades kindergarten through high school, Ms. Smith retired from the school system but remains a strong influence among her peers and young people.

When not teaching or writing, Ms. Smith enjoys dancing, reading, decorating, doing interior design, shopping, walking, biking, horseback riding, cooking, and working with the children's and senior's ministries at her church. She is also an active community leader and consultant with organizations focused on youth development.